First Year on Earth

♥

A Keepsake Book of Our Little Alien

(A Baby Book for Your Adopted Intergalactic Child)

Created by US!

With help from Bayyo and Doccy

Our Little Alien

Life on Earth Before

Adoption Details

Adopted From

Adopted By

Adoption Date

Our Family

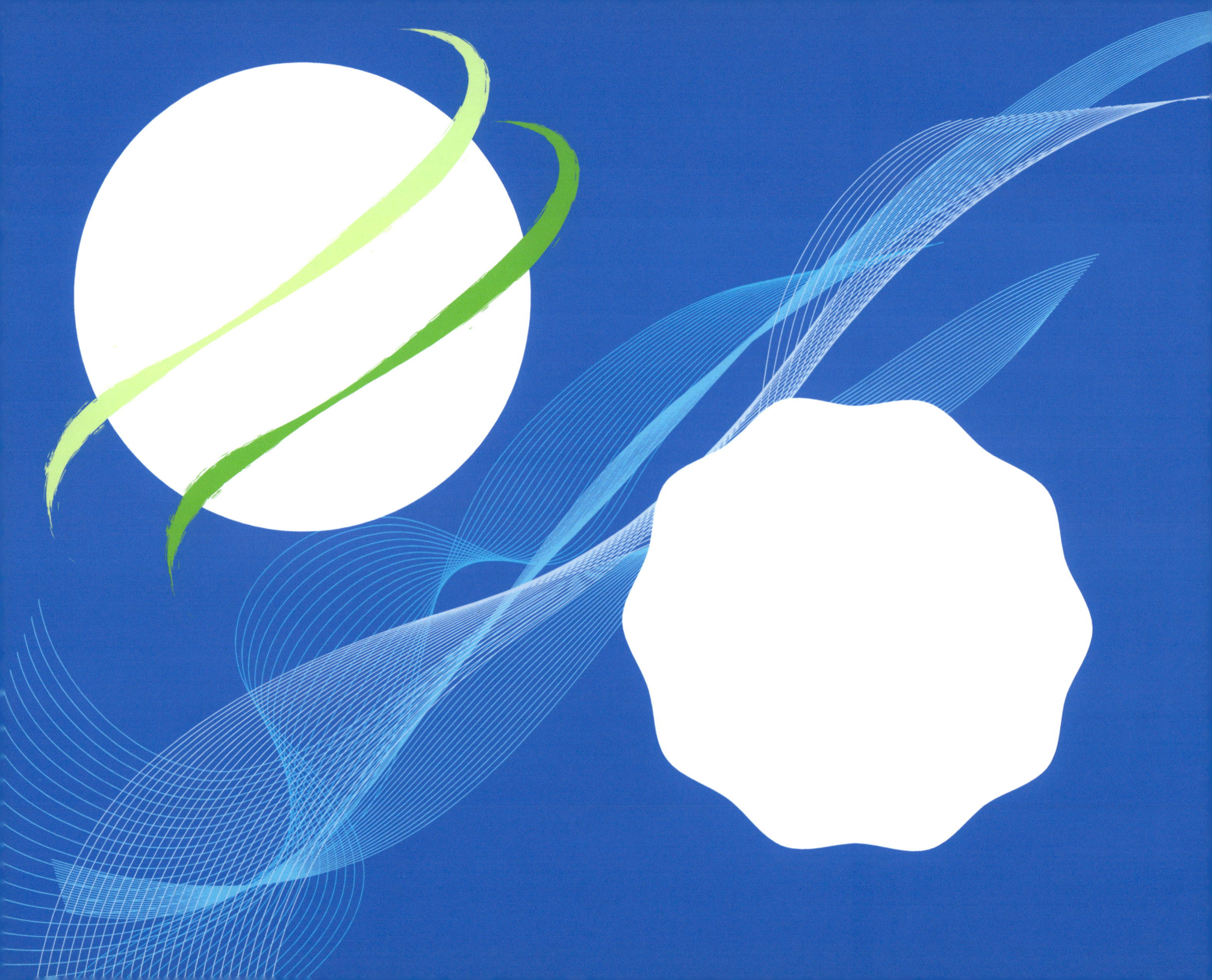

All About You

First word

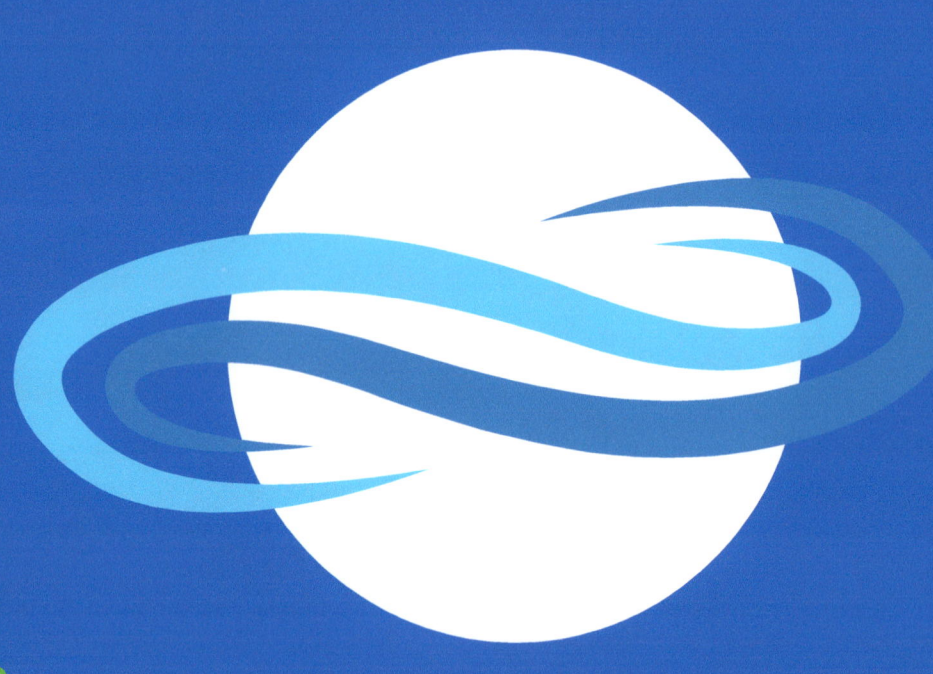

Fave Words

First Outfit

Fave Outfit

First Outing or Adventure

Fave Outings or Adventures

All Your Special Powers

What We Love About You

How you've changed us

Life on Earth Now

ThiS iS US

This is Happiness

This is Love

More Memories

More Memories

Ideas for How To Use this Book

Circles, lines, blank boxes, and other open spaces
are for you! These are the places you create your story!
You can leave the book as it is and create your story aloud,
by talking, or in your imagination all by yourself.
Or You Might Try...
Handwriting * Cutting and Pasting Typed Text *
Photographs * Drawings * Collage * Stickers *
Decorative tape * Postcards * Letters * Stamps *
Embossing * Mementos * Personal Memories * Quotes *
Premade Labels * Lists * Poems * And More!
Not sure if a particular ink or adhesive will work on these
pages? Maybe test it in a small area of the More Memories
pages and give it time to dry to see.
Have Fun!

Page-by-Page Ideas

(Bayyo's Ideas in Quotes, The Rest are Doccy's)

Our Little Alien Page: "Dis is for a piccy pic and name of your smol alien or plushie. Used "Our" and "Us" because you are a family wif your little one & your family is important no matter how big or smol! Plus, you are an "Us" wif everyone else in da whole galaxy who loves little aliens. Lots of us, there are!

If you have many aliens in da family, you can buy a book for each one, or group together in this book, or wait for da Our Galactic Family booky book, wif all da family memories together!"

Doccy here. The Our Little Alien page is designed for an image (pic or drawing) with a name, nickname, or screen name under it. But this is your book! Do whatever you want! Get as creative as you like! Maybe that arch is a window to another world?

Earth Before, Adoption Details & Story, Our Family: "Use piccy pics, drawings, stickers, words, or whatever, fwens! Share da story of how you became an us together!
Fwens, da galaxy needs da stories of how we all found our happy, on our own and together. And this way you can remember forever."

Where We Live: House, Apartment, City, Town, Country, Planet! Whatever you want to say or show about where you live.

All About You: "Every hooman and alien is different and special, fwens! Tell about what makes your little alien who they are."

Firsts and Faves: "Words, snacky snacks, cutey cute...all da best stuff!" These pages are a small ("smol") selection of first and favorite moments from your little alien's first year. And hey, it's fine if your little one hasn't changed much or still prefers their first outfit. Everyone is themselves and that is sci-fi-tastic!

What We Love about You, How You've Changed Us, Life on Earth Now: "Can you even remember what life was like before us, fwen? Did you ever expect so much wonderful? So much wuv? Share here!"

We think you can figure out the rest of the pages on your own, fwens! But if you're looking for ideas, check out our social media pages and hashtags for examples of how other fwens made the books their own. Or share how you've personalized your book! You are also welcome to contact us with questions or fun stuff!

Find us at:
Email: BayyoMail@gmail.com
Insta: @Dr.T_Writes & @BayyoandDoccy
Fwenmail: PO Box 55, Palm Beach, FL 33480 USA
or one of our webpages

Enjoy the Book, Fwens!

Created by
BayYo and Doccy
+
You!

Text and Layout Copyright © BayYo and Doccy
BayYo and Doccy LLC

First Hardcover Edition 2021
ISBN 978 - 1 - 7375420 - 1 - 8

All Rights Reserved. No part of this book may be copied or transmitted in any form or manner including, but not limited to, photography, scanning, photocopying, audio recording, video recording, or digital recording, without written permission from the publishers.

Limited sharing on social media permitted, provided that no reproducible (high def, close-up) images appear and quotations are short and appear with full credit to the authors.

www.ingramcontent.com/pod-product-compliance
Lightning Source LLC
Chambersburg PA
CBHW041108210426

43209CB00063BA/1853